soulsister

shine
Beautiful Inside and Out

Aly Hawkins

Regal

From Gospel Light
Ventura, California, U.S.A.

Gospel Light is a Christian publisher dedicated to serving the local church. We believe God's vision for Gospel Light is to provide church leaders with biblical, user-friendly materials that will help them evangelize, disciple and minister to children, youth and families.

It is our prayer that this Gospel Light resource will help you discover biblical truth for your own life and help you minister to youth. May God richly bless you.

For a free catalog of resources from Gospel Light, please contact your Christian supplier or contact us at 1-800-4-GOSPEL or www.gospellight.com.

PUBLISHING STAFF
William T. Greig, Publisher • **Dr. Elmer L. Towns,** Senior Consulting Publisher • **Alex Field,** Acquisition Editor • **Jessie Minassian,** Assistant Editor • **Bayard Taylor,** M.Div., Senior Editor, Biblical and Theological Issues

ISBN 0-8307-3730-8

table of contents

PART ONE:

creative
me

one: BEAUTIFUL

So God created man in his own image, in the image of God he created him;
male and female he created them.
Genesis 1:27

I don't know about you, but when I read this verse, I find it pretty hard to believe. Me? In God's *image*? Has God really lowered His standards or something?

Most of the time, I feel about as "in God's image" as a ham and cheese sandwich. But my feelings aside, the Bible is pretty clear that when God puffed the breath of life into the first man and woman, it wasn't just oxygen that filled their lungs. God jump-started the hearts of Adam and Eve with a jolt of His very own image—the creative impulse that caused Him to invent them in the first place. Weird, huh? God invented people.

It appears that the creator had so much fun calling the universe into existence, and then decorating it, that He just had to share that joy with somebody. So God didn't stop with giving the first folks free will and intelligence. He went right on ahead and gifted them with an itch to create.

And He didn't stop with good ol' Adam and Eve, either. God's creative fingerprint has been stamped on you and me as well.

The truth is, God hasn't lowered His standards at all. We've lowered ours.

CREATED TO CREATE

We are God's workmanship, created in Christ Jesus to do good works,
which God prepared in advance for us to do.
Ephesians 2:10

In his paraphrase of the Bible called *The Message*, Eugene Peterson rewords Ephesians 2:10 like this: "God does both the making and saving. He creates each of us by Christ Jesus to *join him* in the work he does . . . work we had better be doing" (emphasis added).

Jesus died on the cross and rose again so that we could become coworkers with God in the work He is doing. And that's a bigger job than you might think! The Bible is chock-full of stories about the work God does: rescuing people, answering prayers, healing people, forgiving people, listening to people, revealing truth, reconciling enemies to each other—but the very first work we see God doing at the very beginning of the Bible is *creating*. That's what gets the whole story going!

Have you ever wondered why you love beautiful things? Why your breath catches in your throat at the sight of a rainbow, the sound of rain on the roof or the smell of your favorite flower? Have you ever wondered why you like to draw, cook, write poetry, design clothes or decorate imaginary houses? Isn't it weird that hundreds of songs have been written about sunrises, but people keep writing more? Here's one:

> *God's glory is on tour in the skies,*
> *God-craft on exhibit across the horizon.*
> *Madame Day holds classes every morning,*
> *Professor Night lectures each evening.*
>
> *Their words aren't heard,*
> *their voices aren't recorded,*
> *But their silence fills the earth:*
> *unspoken truth is spoken everywhere.*
>
> *God makes a huge dome*
> *for the sun—a superdome!*
> *The morning sun's a new husband*
> *leaping from his honeymoon bed,*
> *The daybreaking sun an athlete*
> *racing to the tape.*
>
> *That's how God's Word vaults across the skies*
> *from sunrise to sunset,*
> *Melting ice, scorching deserts,*
> *warming hearts to faith.*
>
> —Psalm 19:1-6, *The Message*

Something all human beings have in common is a love for beauty. Sure, beauty is defined differently in various places. In some East African tribes, both men and women stretch their earlobes to hang down to their shoulders. We think it's disgusting; they think it's gorgeous! No matter where you go, you'll find people decorating their surroundings and "improving" their appearance. We are delighted by beauty! Know why? We're fascinated by beauty because God is!

Read the book in the Bible called Song of Songs, or sometimes Song of Solomon. No, really read it. Yes, now! Okay, if you just have time for one chapter, read chapter 7. This chapter is a celebration of the passion between a man and a woman, but it's also a celebration of the passion with which God pursues us, His love! (Giggle-fest Warning: Song of Songs has some pretty sexy word pictures in it, so if you want to read it seriously, *don't* do it at a slumber party!)

Here's another verse from the Bible that reveals how God feels about you:

The LORD your God is with you, he is mighty to save. He will take delight in you, he will quiet you with his love, he will rejoice over you with singing (Zephaniah 3:17).

God thinks you're beautiful. In fact, He *knows* you're beautiful, because He created you that way. God created you to enjoy the beauty He has created, and He created you *as part of* that beauty. And if that wasn't enough, He created you to add your beauty and creativity to His ongoing work!

I DON'T FEEL beautiful

I know, I know. Some days (okay, most days), I don't feel beautiful, either. Some days (most days), I feel like this:

Now go ahead . . . go crazy. Draw what you feel like most days in the space below.

But if it's true that God has created us in His image and delights in us, aren't we kind of making Him out to be a liar, or spitting on the beauty He made (us!), by disagreeing with His standard of beauty? Whoa.

Not good.

If God, the creator of the universe, says that you and I are beautiful, created in His image to delight in and to create more beauty, and we take a long, hard look in the mirror and can't see what He could possibly be talking about, then we're insulting God.

I'm willing to bet that that's something neither one of us wants to keep doing. But how do we stop?

take God at His Word

At some point in time someone has probably said or done something that made you feel less than the beautiful, "in God's image" creation that you are. Try to remember one of these times right now. In my memory, I'm walking down the hallway at my middle school, and Tommy Winter, the hottest guy in sixth grade, smiles at me. I smile back, just as he says, "What's up, Hawkins?" (which is my last name), only when he says "Hawkins" he makes the "Hawk" part into a gagging sound and pretends he's throwing up on my shoes. I did not feel beautiful and "in God's image" at that moment.

Now, as you're watching that memory replay (there may be more than one), make a conscious effort to see Jesus in the picture. The reality is that Jesus was there with you during that memory; you just didn't see Him. At the very same time the cruel thing is said or done, look Jesus in the face and hear Him say to you: "[Your name], I delight in you! Let Me quiet your feelings with My love. And then we'll both sing and dance for joy, because you are re-created in Me to join My Father in doing beautiful things!"

You might feel kind of weird at first. But the Bible is God's Word to us—that means God wants to use its words to speak to you. That's what words are for, right? So let God's Word be the final word in those painful memories you're carrying around in your head.

Use the space below to write out (or draw) a few more memories, and allow Jesus to speak His Words of healing into your spirit.

It's all a matter of whom we choose to believe: God, the creator and lover of all that is beautiful, or Tommy Winter (or whoever has tried to hurt *you* in the past). After a lot of thought, I'm going with God. Honestly, it wasn't that hard of a choice. Tommy Winter wouldn't know beauty if it punched him in the nose (tempting!).

In the next five sessions, we'll take a look at five beautiful areas of your life in which you can shine in God's image. These are areas in which God has uniquely fashioned you to be *you*!

So here we go!

two: passionate

When I was 14, my family moved from the United States to Kenya, which is in East Africa. My parents became missionaries, teaching at a seminary that trained pastors from all over Africa. It was a big change (the understatement of the year!). Eventually I adjusted, and I spent my last three years of high school getting to know people in Kenya, learning about their way of life, their values and their culture.

While I don't think I'll end up back in Kenya to live, my time there gave me a passion for the people of Africa. As we've watched the AIDS crisis explode there in the last several years, my heart always breaks for the families grieving for lost loved ones, the children left without parents and the lack of resources to treat people who are suffering. My interest in Africa's people has led me to invest time, money and prayer in raising the awareness of their condition.

Also when I was 14, I read *The Diary of Anne Frank*, which I highly recommend if you have not already been assigned to read it in school. Anne was a girl in the Netherlands during World War II, and she and her family had to hide in a secret room to avoid being arrested by the Nazis, just for being Jews. They were arrested anyway, after two years in hiding. Anne wrote down her thoughts, feelings, likes, dislikes and fears about growing up during those years of hiding in a diary that was eventually found and published after her death.

Even though Anne and I were born more than 40 years apart, lived on different continents, belonged to different religions and had vastly different experiences, my heart felt that I knew Anne; she was like a friend across time and space. Her story ignited my lifelong passion in bringing peace to people of different racial and religious backgrounds.

As if that wasn't enough activity for one year, when I was 14, I also discovered acting, which quickly became my primary passion. I made my stage debut in a very confusing play about a 6-foot-tall invisible rabbit called *Harvey*, and I played a 60-something-year-old woman named Veta Louise Simmons. It was the role of a lifetime. I got to wear a fake nose. I was brilliant (according to my parents).

I still love to act, and now I like to write plays too. Last Easter, I wrote six miniplays for my church's celebration of Lent, in which characters from the Bible talked about their experiences with Jesus. It was fun!

I'm trying to give you a glimpse into my world because the stuff that I loved at age 14 is the stuff that I'm still passionate about now. Acting and writing also provide me a huge opportunity to reflect God's creative image.

your heartbeat

Be strong and take heart, all you who hope in the LORD.
Psalm 31:24

Delight yourself in the LORD and he will give you the desires of your heart.
Psalm 37:4

So what lights your inner fire? Take 15 to 20 minutes to think about your passions—those things that fill you with a sense of meaning and purpose—and what inspired them (like reading a book or meeting a special person). Write about your inner fire in the space below.

GOD'S HEARTBEAT

And he who searches our hearts knows the mind of the Spirit,
because the Spirit intercedes for the saints in accordance with God's will.
Romans 8:27

Therefore, since through God's mercy we have this ministry, we do not lose heart.
2 Corinthians 4:1

All the things you have listed in the space provided are things God loves about you! He is passionate about your passions and about shining through the things that give your life meaning, purpose and excitement. All you have to do is invite His presence into those areas, and you will find your heart beating with the passion of God.

But how do we do that? Is it really as easy as it sounds? Well, yes and no. Yes, because God is ready, willing and waiting to step in wherever He is invited. No, because sometimes we'd rather keep our interests to ourselves.

Are there times when you have wanted to keep your passions to yourself? I know I've had those times. For many years, acting was one area of my life into which I didn't want God sticking His nose. I wanted to be a *star*, and I knew somewhere down deep inside that if I invited God into my dreams, He might change my heart to reflect His own. This proved to be the correct suspicion, but I've never regretted the choice I made to invite Him in! He knew much better than I did what was best for me. Making a decision to surrender our dreams to our God is *not* the same as just plain giving up, even if it feels like it sometimes.

Think about the risks of inviting God into your passions and interests. What might change if you invited God into your passions? What might stay the same? Try to describe what it might look like to invite God into these areas of your life.

BEAT IT

And in him you too are being built together to become
a dwelling in which God lives by his Spirit.
Ephesians 2:22

The crazy thing about inviting God to share our passions is that we actually become *more* passionate and fired up when we're in His presence, not less! God is the most passionate, exciting and loving being in the whole universe, and when He arrives, He brings all of His passion with Him. Instead of our teeny tiny little hearts beating with our own measly little interests, our hearts can beat in time with the heartbeat of eternity.

This is what we are created for: to reflect God's image. What better way than to have God Himself living on the inside? Have you invited Him in? How has it changed you—what's different? Are there still areas of your heart in which He isn't welcome? Why is it difficult to make that choice? Use the journal space provided to write about these questions in the coming week. When you feel your heartbeat speed up with excitement, take a second to be honest with yourself and invite God's presence into this area of passion. Write down what you discover:

Your passions are part of your beauty. God smiles when He sees your passion, which is a reflection of His passion and love for you. It doesn't matter whether your passion is writing haiku, going bungee jumping, joining student government or rescuing animals—if you invite God into your passionate pursuits, He will infuse you with His own passion and pursue all of your heart until your delight is in Him.

three: UNIQUE

There are different kinds of gifts, but the same Spirit. There are different kinds of service,
but the same LORD. There are different kinds of working, but the same God works all of them
in all men. Now to each one the manifestation of the Spirit is given for the common good.
1 Corinthians 12:4-7

M.O. stands for the Latin phrase *modus operandi*, which means "mode of operation."
(Didn't know you'd be learning Latin today, did you?) It's a slang word that refers to the way
someone does life; in other words, his or her personality. According to David Keirsey, there are
four basic personality types, with some variation even within one type. The main four are
Rationals, Artisans, Idealists and Guardians.[1] In this chapter, we'll take a look at each type and
see how God has made each one to be a unique reflection of His image. For the record: *There
are no bad personality types*. And these are not hard and fast lines—many personalities encompass
more than one type. Each and every personality has something special to offer, and a way to shine
God's image in a way the others can't. Your personality is a beautiful part of a beautiful you.

You'll probably be able to discover your personality just from reading the descriptions, but I
encourage you to take a "type test" when you get a chance. You can take a free test online at
www.advisorteam.com, or you can get a book called *Please Understand Me II*, by David Keirsey,
which has a lot more information about the four personality types.

rationals: knowledge seekers

The heart of the discerning acquires knowledge; the ears of the wise seek it out.
Proverbs 18:15

Bill Gates, the founder of Microsoft Corporation and one of the richest men in the world, is a
Rational. So is Margaret Thatcher, England's first female prime minister. The writer and humorist
Mark Twain, who wrote *The Adventures of Tom Sawyer* and *Innocents Abroad*, was a Rational,
as well as Walt Disney, the man who founded an entertainment empire on a squeaky-voiced
money machine named Mickey Mouse.

As you might expect, Rationals are rational, the meaning of which is "having reason or understanding."[2] They love words like "strategy," "analysis," "planning" and "invention," and they take extraordinary pleasure in collecting data. They feel best about themselves when they are strong willed and competent, and they seek recognition for achievement and excellence.

My mom is a Rational. She has a Ph.D. in sociology, loves the military lawyer TV show JAG and tells stories with as many details as possible, because to her, the details are just as important as the actual point. Mom is smart. She can use words like "excoriating" and "rudimentary" and make them sound cool, and she has an amazing ability to figure out the very best way to do anything. This means she is right most of the time, a fact that was incredibly frustrating when I was growing up!

Rationals are uniquely gifted to reflect God's creative image through invention (creating brand-new things) and innovation (improving old things). They have the mysterious ability to see how things work and then to figure out how they might work better. This is important! Where would we be without John Wycliffe, the smart, visionary guy who decided to translate the Bible into English? You and I would have to learn a lot more Latin than modus operandi, that's for sure! Or what would the United States look like without Abraham Lincoln, who could see that unity was the only way the United States could survive? We wouldn't be united at all! Both of these men reflected God's image through their personalities, and they changed the world in the process.

🖝 **Is Rational your personality type? If not, do you know someone who is a Rational? Use the space provided to describe a Rational—either yourself or someone you know.**

🖝 **If Rational is your personality type, take a few minutes to think about how you relate to people. How do you think other people see you (smart, arrogant, confident, boring, friendly or cold)? Why?**

artisans: impact seekers

I myself am convinced, my brothers, that you yourselves are full of goodness, complete in knowledge and competent to instruct one another.
Romans 15:14

Madonna is an Artisan. Other Artisans include filmmaker Steven Spielberg; retired basketball star Michael Jordan; singer, movie director, producer and comedienne Barbra Streisand; and Donald Trump, the boss with the weird hair on the TV show *The Apprentice*. Elvis Presley and Marilyn Monroe were both Artisans, as well as Franklin D. Roosevelt, who was president of the United States during World War II.

Perhaps you've guessed that many Artisans like working in the arts. Artisans love words like "display," "compose," "promote" and "persuade," and they hunger to make a lasting impact on others. They feel best about themselves when they are fluid and adaptable, and they seek recognition for being daring and bold.

My friend Chad is an Artisan. Among my friends who are musicians, he is one of the most talented singer-songwriters I know. He is hilarious and electrifying in front of a crowd, but what really gets Chad out of bed every morning is the idea that he has something to share that will influence people—that will truly change them. You can see it in the songs he writes, which look at something familiar and then view it through a unique word picture. Like this lyric from a song he wrote titled "Drenched," which is about the third person of the Trinity, the Holy Spirit:

> I'm wading out so far that my feet can't touch.
> I'm swimming where the water churns white.
> I'm wading out so far that my feet can't touch.
> I'm drinking in the water of Life.[3]

Artisans are uniquely gifted to reflect God's creative image through artistry and influence. Nothing changes people so quickly as good art, which invites both the mind and heart to interact and engage with new ideas. Can you remember hearing a life-changing song for the first time? Or seeing a movie that totally changed your point of view? Or hearing a speech or sermon that opened your mind? This is the gift of the Artisan, who speaks to both our emotions and our intellect to change our lives.

💬 Is Artisan your personality type? If not, do you know someone who is an Artisan? Use the space provided to describe an Artisan—either yourself or someone you know.

💬 If Artisan is your personality type, take a few minutes to think about how you relate to people. How do you think other people see you (brilliant, bold, careless, unkind, ingenious or unconventional)? Why?

idealists: identity seekers

Whoever finds his life will lose it, and whoever loses his life for my sake will find it.
Matthew 10:39

Mahatma Gandhi, the revolutionary who helped win India's independence from Britain through nonviolent resistance, was an Idealist. So was Eleanor Roosevelt and the famous Russian novelist Leo Tolstoy, who wrote the brilliant (and very long) novel *War and Peace*. Oprah Winfrey is an Idealist, and so is world-renowned evangelist Billy Graham.

Idealists are driven by ideas, and they look at life as a meaningful journey of discovery. Idealists love words like "personal," "meaningful," "connection" and "intuition," and they long for deep and significant relationships. They feel best about themselves when they are generous and authentic, and they seek recognition for their passion and integrity.

I am an Idealist. I want to connect with people, to really know what they're about and to let them know I genuinely care about them. To me, everything is about "personal growth," so I'm obsessed with psychology, spirituality and group dynamics. My mind is constantly looking for new ideas. Consequently, I love to read, dialogue with a wide variety of people, watch documentary TV (like the History Channel) and travel to new places. I'm also passionate about "causes," since I hate to see people hurting.

Idealists are uniquely gifted to reflect God's creative image through empathy (feeling the pain of others) and advocacy (speaking up for people who need help). God created people to connect with and care about each other, and Idealists are the ones who remind everybody else! Idealists can find creative ways to care for the people around them in their day-to-day relationships, and they can also challenge others to the same high standard of love.

Are you an Idealist? If not, do you know someone who is? Use the space provided to describe an Idealist—either yourself or someone you know.

If Idealist is your personality type, take a few minutes to think about how you relate to people. How do you think other people see you (tenderhearted, naïve, optimistic, unrealistic or determined)? Why?

guardians:
security seekers

I will lie down and sleep in peace, for you alone, O LORD, make me dwell in safety.
Psalm 4:8

George Washington, the first president of the United States, was a Guardian. So was Mother Teresa of Calcutta, who started the Missionaries of Charity (a Catholic community that cares for the poorest of the poor around the world). The Queen of England, Elizabeth II, is a Guardian, as well as Barbara Walters, the first successful United States network newswoman.

Guardians make sure that whatever happens goes well and doesn't fall apart at the last minute. They love words like "protect," "supervise," "reliability" and "membership," and they want to belong to the group. Guardians feel best about themselves when they do good deeds, and they seek recognition for doing the right thing.

My friend Lori is a Guardian. She and I started a girls' Bible study group a couple years ago, and Lori kept running lists of everything that needed deciding. She'd mark the items on her list "done," "in process" or "still to be completed." It wasn't until all the details had been hashed through that she could relax and enjoy herself. She was awesome! We never would have made any progress in organizing ourselves if she wasn't there with her lists, letting us know what needed to be done every week.

Guardians are uniquely gifted to reflect God's creative image through cooperation and protection. Guardians like being part of a group, and they recognize that much more can be accomplished when people work together, so they compromise easily—except when it comes to doing the right thing! They want to protect others from harm, even if it means putting themselves at risk. Guardians are everyday heroes!

Is Guardian your personality type? If not, do you know someone who is a Guardian? Use the space below to describe a Guardian—either you or someone you know.

💬 **If Guardian is your personality type, take a few minutes to think about how you relate to people. How do you think other people see you (organized, cautious, concerned, principled or thoughtful)? Why?**

your personality type
is too cool

Now go back and review whichever personality type best describes you. If you have trouble pinpointing just one, pick two personality types from those discussed in this session. Now use the space below to brainstorm ideas about how you can reflect God's image through your personality type. Once you've got your list, get together with a group of friends who have different personality types and share your ideas. Be creative!

Whatever your personality type, you can creatively reflect God's image in you. And as you begin to identify other people's personality types, you can appreciate how they are uniquely reflecting God's image, too! Cherish the beauty you have to offer in your personality—God does!

Notes

1. David Keirsey, "Temperament: Different Drums, Different Drummers," *Keirsey Temperament and Character Website*, February 14, 2004. http://www.keirsey.com (accessed December 14, 2004).
2. *Merriam-Webster's Collegiate Dictionary*, 11th ed., s.v. "rational."
3. Chad C. Reisser, "Drenched," copyright 1999, all rights reserved. Used by permission.

four: TALENTED

I testify that they gave as much as they were able, and even beyond their ability. Entirely on their own, they urgently pleaded with us for the privilege of sharing in this service to the saints.

2 Corinthians 8:3-4

In basketball, you got game. In rap, you got rhyme. In dancing, you got skills. Everybody's got something. But even if you don't got what you think you want, you do have a ton of ability, talent and skill that make up a big part of the image of God in you. And even if you are not—and never will be—the very best at whatever your ability is, your beauty will shine if you are ready and willing to use your skills creatively.

Taking an inventory of your abilities is a bigger job than it might seem. We sell ourselves short way too often! We all have one or two big things that we're good at, but we don't often think of the small stuff, such as reading, writing, typing, driving (if you're old enough), riding a bike, doing long division, cleaning the bathroom, baking, playing miniature golf, shining shoes, sewing on buttons, running, gardening, reading maps, remembering numbers and dates, surfing, snow skiing, alphabetizing, folding napkins in designs, drawing, using a thesaurus, talking in sign language, crocheting, beating your older sister in Scrabble, memorizing baseball stats, installing new software on your computer, telling stories to children, changing light bulbs, taking pictures, text messaging, caring for your pet, doing origami, debating, making funny posters for school events, rock climbing and, of course, talking on the phone.

All of these activities require a certain amount of skill (okay, talking on the phone doesn't take a lot of skill, but there is something to be said for endurance), and each presents an opportunity to shine God's creative image.

THE TALENTS

To one he gave five talents of money, to another two talents, and to another one talent, each according to his ability.

Matthew 25:15

Jesus told a lot of parables, which are stories about familiar things (such as bread, seeds or animals) that make a point about unfamiliar things, usually the kingdom of God. The time in history that Jesus walked the earth was in some ways very different from ours, so the stories Jesus told those people were about things that were familiar to them but probably aren't very familiar to us. That's okay though, since we have imaginations and can try to understand from their point of view.

Take a few minutes and read the parable of the talents in Matthew 25:14-30; then respond to the questions in the spaces provided. **Note:** A "talent" in Jesus' day was quite a bit of money—more than $1,000—which, in those days would have amounted to about 15 years of a working man's wages!

- **How did the parable make you feel? Angry? Pleased? Envious?**

- **The master in the story who owned all the talents represents God. Do you think about your talents as being owned by God? Why or why not?**

- **Why do you think the man who got one talent dug a hole and hid it? Have you ever felt the same way?**

- **Do you think it's fair that the servant who had the most talents got the one talent from the servant who did nothing with his? Why or why not?**

I'm sure we all have different reactions to this parable, but I gotta tell you, it makes me angry! It just seems so unfair! I mean, the poor loser who only got one talent was probably scared out of his mind about losing it or screwing up—and he got punished! It's not fair!

GOD'S IDEA OF FAIR

Whoever does not love does not know God, because God is love.
1 John 4:8

It may be a bitter pill to swallow, but God's idea of fairness is way different from ours. I often define fair as "what won't hurt me and what will bring me pleasure." God defines fair as any situation or circumstance that gives me an opportunity to reflect His image—which can sometimes hurt like fire and be about as pleasurable as a picnic in poison ivy. The deal is that God imprints His creative image onto us, but in order to shine that image the very brightest that it can shine, we have to learn to grow up into God's character. The character of God is what makes His image glow.

So what does that look like? Well, 1 John 4:8 pretty much sums it up. God is love. "Love" is a word that gets tossed around a lot, but the essence of love can be found in a word that occasionally (in my most selfish moments) brings a chill to my heart: "sacrifice."

Romans 5:8 says that sacrifice, specifically the sacrifice of Jesus, is the number one way God demonstrates His love. "God demonstrates his own love for us in this: While we were still sinners, Christ died for us." How amazing is that? The ultimate way to show love is through sacrifice.

So when God gives us a chance to sacrifice—to give up what we really want for the sake of love—He expects us to take it. Would you expect any less, after giving up your son? Would it be "fair" to expect people who have been imprinted with the image of God to act like it?

THE TALENTS:
PART TWO

So let's get back to the parable of the talents.

💬 **In light of our new perspective on how God defines fairness, why do you think the master in the story was so angry with the servant who did nothing with his talent?**

First John 4:18 says this: "There is no fear in love. But perfect love drives out fear, because fear has to do with punishment. The one who fears is not made perfect in love."

💬 **If the one-talent servant had acted out of love instead of fear, what do you think he would have done differently?**

your talents, your love

But what does this mean for us? Well, we have all been given some talents. Some are big, some are small, and some are a bit ridiculous. I have a friend who can tie two cherry stems together, using only her tongue. I don't think she should list this on her résumé when she goes out to look for a job, but she possesses a unique talent nonetheless. God gives us talents so that we can shine His image creatively. If we're too afraid and bury them underground so that we don't screw up, like the one-talent servant in the parable, we're missing the point of having talents in the first place! *They are meant to shine.*

Letting our talents shine may involve a bit of risk. That's okay—God loves risk takers! Think about it from His point of view: Would you rather see someone overwhelmed by your love, determined to reflect your image and character, step out boldly and take a risk, or would you rather see someone play it safe, afraid that your love won't be enough if they mess up? I thought you'd say that. So let's get down to business and figure out what talents God has given us so that we can begin letting them shine.

Use the journaling space provided to take an inventory of *all* your talents, abilities and skills. Make sure you give yourself some time with this "assignment." You won't believe how many talents you have waiting for some attention. You may need to carry this book around with you for a few days to jot down talents you can't think of right now. When you feel like you have a fairly complete list, go through them one at a time and rate yourself on how well you're letting each talent shine (1 = I've seen broken lightbulbs produce more glow, 10 = Shining like a bald head in a heat wave).

As you rate each one, ask yourself the following questions:

- Are you investing the necessary time to develop your talent?
- Are you using that skill to show God and people around you that you love them?
- Have you buried this talent and need to dig it up, dust it off and shine it to sheen?

Okay, have at it!

When you use your abilities with love, the creative image of God will light you up like a Christmas tree. There is nothing more beautiful than a loving, spiritually-charged woman using her abilities to create something—and you can be that woman!

five: fruitful

There are different kinds of gifts, but the same Spirit. There are different kinds of service, but the same LORD. There are different kinds of working, but the same God works all of them in all men.
1 Corinthians 12:4-6

But the fruit of the Spirit is love, joy, peace, patience, kindness, goodness, faithfulness, gentleness and self control.
Galatians 5:22-23

As you seek to shine God's image every day, remember that you have a secret weapon. No, it's not an 1800-watt hair dryer. It's not even your "God's Girl" lip gloss. Your secret weapon is better than that—it's the Holy Spirit.

As Christians, we believe that God exists as one God in three persons: the Father, the Son and the Holy Spirit. These three persons make up the Trinity. The Trinity is a mystery, which means that there are elements about it that are far beyond human understanding. Anyone who tells you that they "totally get" the Trinity is delusional. Just because it's a mystery doesn't mean it's not worth studying. Unfortunately, I don't have the space here to dig into trinitarian theology and explicate its implications for a twenty-first century hermeneutic. And I'll bet you're glad, after that sentence! But we *can* go over some basics.

For today, it's enough to know that the Holy Spirit is the One that Jesus promised when He said, "I will ask the Father, and he will give you another Counselor to be with you forever" (John 14:16) and "The Holy Spirit . . . will teach you all things and will remind you of everything I have said to you" (John 14:26). The Holy Spirit is the person of God who actually lives with us, lives in us and reminds us who we are in Jesus, teaching us how to live as God's image bearers. *How cool is that?* We don't have to guess what it looks like to shine God's image; God Himself is with us and in us, willing to teach us how!

Sometimes you can feel the Holy Spirit's presence. Other times, not so much. But that doesn't mean that you're on your own! You can see the evidence of the Holy Spirit's presence in your life by the fruit you bear—the good stuff you're growing and giving away. Take another look at Galatians 5:22-23. If you have ripening love, joy, peace, patience and other fruit falling off your branches—so much that you're giving them away at every opportunity—you can be sure that the Holy Spirit is working in you so that you shine God's image.

Every Jesus follower should see these fruit ripening in his or her life, but it's a lifelong process, a process that none of us will get right 100 percent of the time. Just when I think I've mastered joy, a big old lack of self-control sneaks up to bite me (and impatience is not far behind!). But right behind them is the presence of the Holy Spirit, reminding me of Jesus and teaching me how to be more like Him. I can't lose!

How are you doing with your fruit growing? Next to each fruit of the Spirit listed in the spaces provided, evaluate its ripeness in your life. How's love coming along? Is kindness looking a little green? If you're not sure how you're doing, ask someone in your family—they see you at your best and at your worst!

- **Love**

- **Joy**

- **Peace**

- **Patience**

- **Kindness**

- **Goodness**

- **Faithfulness**

- **Self-control**

Just in case you missed it the first time, *all* Jesus followers should be growing *all* the fruit of the Spirit. We don't get to pick the easy ones—wait, there are no easy ones! The fruit of the Spirit are not optional.

It's easy to confuse the fruit of the Spirit with "spiritual gifts." They are totally different. How? Glad you asked.

Spiritual gifts are special powers (kind of like superpowers, but they come from the Holy Spirit, not from aliens or strange cosmic happenings) that God gives to each Jesus follower so that we can be a part of God's work on Earth. Our spiritual gifts can encourage other Jesus followers, challenge them, assist them and motivate them to follow Jesus more closely. Our spiritual gifts can also encourage, assist, challenge and motivate those who don't know Jesus to find out what it means to be bearers of God's image.

your gift is present

Now to each one the manifestation of the Spirit is given for the common good. All these are the work of one and the same Spirit, and he gives them to each one, just as he determines.
1 Corinthians 12:7,11

Now, just like Spider-Man doesn't have the ability to fly, and Superman doesn't have web-spinning ability, none of us has all the spiritual gifts. In fact, most of us have one or two gifts that stand out from the others. And if you don't think you have one, you're wrong! Discovering your spiritual gifts can be a long process, and sometimes it won't be obvious until you're an adult, but God has blessed each believer with unique gifts. And the more you know about your gifts, the more you will understand how you can shine God's image in your own unique and beautiful way.

On the next few pages you will find a "gifts inventory" that will help you discover your gift or gifts. Follow the instructions for the inventory, and then we'll explore each of the gifts and brainstorm ways to use them. By the way, this inventory is not a complete list of all the spiritual gifts, nor is it the final word on your spiritual gifts. But it can be an indicator of what your gifts may be. As you practice using some of these gifts and receive good counsel and advice from other Jesus followers—like a "big sis," youth leader or pastor—you will have a clearer understanding of your spiritual gifts. And for the record, there are no bad spiritual gifts. God is not in the habit of giving lame gifts, so if yours seems less glamorous or flashy than others, you didn't get ripped off. God has in His mind a beautiful way for you to reflect His image, and it will be an adventure to discover it!

GIFTS INVENTORY

For each statement below, rate yourself 1 to 4 on the scoring sheet on page 40. Enter 4 for "always true," 3 for "sometimes true," 2 for "rarely true" or 1 for "not at all true." Don't enter what you think *should* be true; be honest with yourself. (I always want to put a 4 when I get to "I love helping others be the best they can be, even if I don't get recognition," but I have to put a 1 instead.) After you finish marking your answers to the following questions on the scoring sheet (which should take 10 to 15 minutes), you will find instructions on how to score it. Okay, here we go . . .

Note: You may belong to a church that also recognizes gifts such as healing, miracles, speaking in tongues, prophecy, apostleship, pastoring or exorcism. If this is the case, you should ask your youth leader or pastor for information on these gifts.

1.   I am good at organizing information, people and resources to reach a goal.

2.   I enjoy learning all I can about many different subjects and issues.

3.   I often understand what can be done to solve a difficult problem.

4.   People have told me that I am good at explaining hard topics.

5.   I love to share my relationship with God with people who don't know Jesus.

6.   I enjoy taking care of little details that no one else has time to do.

7.   I speak up when I feel that someone is getting off track in their spiritual life.

8.   I love to worship God through music.

9.   I am good at making beautiful things when I draw, sculpt, write or paint.

10.   I enjoy sharing my money, and I don't worry that I won't have enough.

11.   I love helping others be the best they can be, even if I don't get recognition.

12.   I can usually tell whether a teacher or preacher is speaking the truth.

13.   When someone is hurting, I hurt too, and I always try to help.

14.   I invite people over to my house when they seem lonely.

15.   When I'm in a group, people naturally follow me.

16.   I like to figure out the best and most efficient way of doing things.

17. I can remember things I've learned at different times and connect them in my mind.

18. People often seek my advice when they don't know what to do.

19. I get excited about explaining God's Word and telling others how it is influencing my life.

20. I have a strong desire to tell people about Jesus.

21. I enjoy meeting other people's needs, no matter how small the task.

22. When I think someone isn't doing his or her best, I challenge that person to do better.

23. People tell me that my music has helped them sense God's presence.

24. I can design and build whatever is needed.

25. When I see that someone has a need, I share whatever I have to meet it.

26. I like to assist leaders with little things so that they will have time for bigger things.

27. I can spot a spiritual phony a mile away.

28. I have trouble holding back tears when someone else is crying.

29. I enjoy making people feel comfortable and at home.

30. When I ask someone to do something, that person is usually happy to do it.

31. I often see abilities and gifts in others and how they can minister effectively.

32. I don't have to try very hard to remember information.

33. People usually follow the advice that I give, and they are glad they did.

34. When I speak, people listen and are interested in what I have to say.

35. I love getting to know unbelievers so that I can show them God's love.

36. I like to make other people happy by helping them complete their tasks.

37. I challenge people to grow spiritually without condemning them.

38. When I sing or play music, others are inspired to seek God.

39. I like to work creatively with my hands.

40. When I have something that someone else needs, I don't hesitate to give it to him or her.

41. Nothing makes me happier than helping someone else live up to God's image.

42. People come to me for help when they need to tell the difference between the truth and a lie.

43. I like to make friends with those who are usually ignored by others.

44. People always feel welcome when they come to my house.

45. I can guide a group of people to accomplish a particular goal.

SCORING SHEET

			Total	Spiritual Gift
1.	16.	31.		Administration
2.	17.	32.		Knowledge
3.	18.	33.		Wisdom
4.	19.	34.		Teaching
5.	20.	35.		Evangelism
6.	21.	36.		Serving
7.	22.	37.		Exhortation
8.	23.	38.		Music/Worship
9.	24.	39.		Art/Craftsmanship
10.	25.	40.		Giving
11.	26.	41.		Helping
12.	27.	42.		Discernment
13.	28.	43.		Mercy
14.	29.	44.		Hospititality
15.	30.	45.		Leadership

To score the inventory, add across the row to the "Total" column. (For example, add your answers for 1, 16 and 31.) You should come up with a number between 3 and 12. When you have done this for each row, circle the one or two (or three if they're close) gifts with the highest number. These are most likely your primary spiritual gifts.

Now that you've got a general idea of some of your spiritual gifts, let's take a look at what each one means. Remember that all of these gifts are given to help us reflect God's image and help each other. You can add "to reflect God's image" at the end of each definition, if it will help you remember!

Administration is the gift of organizing people and resources to accomplish a goal.
Art/Craftsmanship is the gift of hands-on creativity (like building or making crafts).
Discernment is the gift of knowing whether something (like a teaching) is from God.
Evangelism is the gift of sharing God's good news with people who don't know Jesus.
Exhortation is the gift of encouraging or challenging others to draw closer to God.
Giving is the gift of sharing resources (financial, spiritual or physical) generously.
Helping is the gift of investing in the gifts of other followers of Jesus.
Hospitality is the gift of welcoming people who need to be taken care of.
Knowledge is the gift of learning information and analyzing ideas.
Leadership is the gift of setting goals and motivating people to accomplish them.
Mercy is the gift of feeling other people's suffering and trying to help.
Music/Worship is the gift of musical creativity.
Serving is the gift of working behind the scenes to accomplish a group's goal.
Teaching is the gift of communicating information and ideas (especially relating to God's truth) so that others can learn.
Wisdom is the gift of knowing how to apply knowledge to people's needs.

Congratulations! You've passed your crash course on the fruit of the Spirit and spiritual gifts. I hope this is just the beginning of an exciting adventure for you, as you discover how you can shine God's beautiful and creative image with the help of the Holy Spirit's presence in your life.

How can you work on growing more fruit in your life and better use your gifts to reflect God's image? Use the space provided to brainstorm several ideas.

Now get together with a couple friends or a "big sis" to exchange ideas and encourage each other to grow the fruit of the Spirit and strengthen your spiritual gifts!

6 six: experienced

Grow in the grace and knowledge of our LORD and Savior Jesus Christ.
To him be glory both now and forever!
2 Peter 3:18

When you were born, your personality, your abilities, your interests and your God-given desire to create beauty were already planted inside of you, like tiny seeds. Even though all these seeds were inside of you, it is the life you've lived *since* your birth that has truly grown you into who you are. You came into this world as a completely unique bundle of God's image, but it would have been impossible to shine that image without experiencing anything! Your everyday experiences combine to help shape your thoughts, feelings, values and relationships.

I don't want to be too broad in my definition, but your experiences include everything that's ever happened to you and every person you've ever met in your entire life. (That really narrows it down, doesn't it?) As insignificant as some of these situations and people may seem, they have shaped and are continuing to shape the way you shine God's beautiful image.

Take a few minutes and remember *a good experience* that later turned out to be really important. Here's mine: When I was in first grade, I wrote a poem for my mom for Mother's Day. Up until then, I knew that I loved to read more than anything else in the world, but I didn't know that I could write creatively. The poem was pretty good for a six-year-old (I'm probably a little biased), but what really left an impression was the way Mom treated that poem like it was the second coming of Shakespeare. She laminated it and has kept it in her Bible for more than . . . well, a really long time. More than anything else that I've experienced, I can point to that poem, and Mom's celebration of it, as the moment I realized I wanted to write.

💬 **Do you remember a good experience that left an impression on you? Write about it in the space below.**

life ain't all sunshine and roses

*He causes his sun to rise on the evil and the good,
and sends rain on the righteous and the unrighteous.*
Matthew 5:45

Obviously, some experiences are better than others. It would be great if we could edit or delete all the *bad experiences*, but the truth is, the bad ones shape us and give us an opportunity to shine just as much as the good ones (sometimes more, actually).

Some of those bad experiences turn out to be really important later. Here's mine: When I was in second grade, my dad was the assistant pastor at a little church where one of the older ladies (let's call her "Sister Dina") was mean and manipulative. My parents tried to keep my brother and me away from her as much as possible, but one night both Mom and Dad had to be in a meeting and couldn't get a babysitter, so we went along to play in my dad's office. After about a half hour, Sister Dina came in and accused Tim (my brother) and me of wrecking the church nursery. She grabbed us each by the arm and dragged us down the hall, where we could see that all the toys had been taken out and strewn all over the floor. I looked up at her and started to say that Tim and I hadn't done it, but she slapped me across the face before I could get the words out. I was shocked! Then Sister Dina looked me right in the eye and said, "You clean this up right now, and if you tell anyone about this, I'll make sure your dad loses his job." I was so scared my dad would get fired and it would be my fault that I didn't tell anyone for years. It was awful.

That one bad experience made a mark on my seven-year-old heart that still has not been completely erased. And I'm not alone. I've met countless girls who have been mistreated or abused in a way that has made a mark on their hearts, and others who have helplessly watched their families break apart through divorce or death. Other girls have an illness or an emotional imbalance (such as depression or anxiety) that has made it hard for them to live a "normal" life, while still others are dealing with an eating disorder, such as anorexia or bulimia. There are many bad experiences that can leave marks on girls' hearts.

Do you remember a bad experience that left its mark on you? Write about it in the space below.

redeeming
the bad for good

We wait for the blessed hope—the glorious appearing of our great God and Savior, Jesus Christ, who gave himself for us to redeem us from all wickedness and to purify for himself a people that are his very own, eager to do what is good.
Titus 2:13-14

If you were to look up the word "redeem" in a dictionary, you'd find that it means "to release from blame or debt; to free from the consequences of sin." This is how we hear it used at church all the time. But there is another definition of the word "redeem" that helps us understand how bad experiences can be turned into an opportunity to shine God's image. Redeem also means "to offset the bad effect of; to make worthwhile."[1] In other words, the bad gets turned to good.

In Titus 2:13-14, Paul praises Jesus for redeeming us, not just from our own wickedness, but from *all* wickedness—the wickedness of other people and the wickedness of situations outside our control. This means that Jesus, through His death and resurrection, can turn the bad of our experiences into good, making them *worthwhile*.

You might be asking yourself right now, *How in the name of Mike can Jesus possibly take my bad experience and make it good? There's no way that what I've gone through could ever be worthwhile!* You might be thinking that no good can come of your uncle molesting you, your dad moving out of your house, the scary panic attacks you've had or the gossipy friends who spread lies behind your back. And I hear you, babe. When you're in the middle of a bad experience, it really seems like nothing in the world could make it good—not even Jesus. But God has never been confined to what seems certain to us.

beginnging to heal

Often, we must go through a long healing process before we see how Jesus redeems our bad experiences. I know that's been the case for me. It took me almost 15 years to forgive Sister Dina, and I am still healing, but I am beginning to see how Jesus is redeeming that bad experience and making it worthwhile. In the last several years, I have gotten to know other girls who were hurt by someone in their church, and were affected in their faith. I have been able to share their pain and encourage them in a way that I never could have without experiencing abuse myself. It's weird to be thankful for something so horrible, but as I continue to heal, I am "eager to do what is good" (Titus 2:14) with my bad experience.

Actually talking to someone about my memories of Sister Dina started the healing process for me. This might sound pretty basic, but for many girls in need of redemption and healing, this is the hardest step. One of the verses quoted most often by people who don't want to share their hurts is, "I can do everything through [Christ] who gives me strength" (Philippians 4:13). But sometimes people forget to read the very next verse: "Yet it was good of you to share in my troubles." In this letter to the Christians in Philippi, Paul talks about trusting Jesus during hard times, but he also makes a point to thank the Philippians for sharing his hard times so that he didn't have to face them alone.

If you have had bad experiences that have left a painful mark on your heart, you don't have to bear that burden alone. In fact, the longer you wait to share your hurts and start the healing process, the longer that process will take. If we don't share our hurts, our minds can actually start to play tricks on us, distorting or burying hurtful memories until we can't even see the damage anymore—but it's still there. The only way Jesus can redeem the bad and turn it to good is if we first allow Him to expose the truth about the bad.

Have you talked to someone like a "big sis," parent, youth leader or pastor about your bad experience? If you haven't, I hope you'll do so this week. If you're not sure how to begin, use the space below to write about the experience—how you felt about it, when it happened and how you feel about it now—and then bring this book with you when you meet. This should be enough to get the conversation started.

💬 **This is what happened:**

💬 **This is how I felt about it when it happened:**

💬 **This is how I feel about it now:**

💬 **I can tell it still affects me because:**

shine the image,
share the experience

For God did not give us a spirit of timidity, but a spirit of power, of love and of self-discipline. So do not be ashamed to testify about our LORD . . . But join with me in suffering for the gospel, by the power of God, who has saved us and called us to a holy life—not because of anything we have done but because of his own purpose and grace.

2 Timothy 1:7-9

Our biggest opportunity to shine God's image through our experiences comes when we are willing to share them. This goes for both the good and the bad! When times are good, we can shine God's image by being grateful and sharing our blessings with others. When times are bad, we can shine God's image by being honest and sharing our hurts with others. Romans 12:15 says, "Rejoice with those who rejoice; mourn with those who mourn." Experiences are what bring people together, and God is all about bringing people together!

A big part of shining God's beauty is also sharing other people's experiences. Sharing in someone's joy or sorrow shines God's love like nothing else!

● **Brainstorm ways that you can share joy with those who are joyful and share sadness with those who are sad.**

image commitment

So you're imprinted with God's creative image. (I hope that rings a bell!) You are truly unique and beautiful; you have been chosen by God to reflect a part of Himself that no one else can.

So are you ready to shine? If you are, grab some colored paper and a glitter pen and copy down the covenant (promise) below. Put it on your mirror or in your locker where you'll see it every day, reminding yourself whose image you carry, and promising Him that you'll shine for His glory.

> God, I'm so grateful that I am imprinted with Your creative image! With the presence of the Holy Spirit in my life, teach me how to shine beautifully in my interests, my personality, my abilities, my gifts and my experiences. I promise You to do my best to shine brighter and brighter each day.

Signed _____ Date _____

Note

1. *Merriam-Webster's Collegiate Dictionary*, 11th ed., s.v. "redeem."

part two:

beautiful me

seven: created

When I was in eighth or ninth grade, I saw a really crazy video in science class. It was a course in anatomy, which is the study of the human body, and the video was an X ray of someone eating. Instead of taking a still-picture X ray, like the kind you get at the hospital when you break your arm, this was a live-action X ray that recorded all of the skeleton's movement during the process of chewing and swallowing. All that was visible were bones and food, in a ghostly greenish light. It was creepy! For some reason that image—of teeth and jaws chomping away, and of the food slithering its way down the throat and past the ribs to settle in front of the spine—was branded in my memory forever.

Even now, sometimes, I see my hands typing on the computer or feel my toes flexing in my shoes and I get kind of freaked out. Having a skeleton is weird, man—all those bones hidden under my skin and muscle like some hair-raising Halloween *monster*, ready to jump out at any minute! And yet, what would I do without a skeleton? Slip down to the floor in a pool of mush, that's what! I need these bones, just as I need my muscles, veins, lungs, heart, skin, brain—you get the picture.

What would life be like without these things? Use the box below to draw a picture of yourself without one or more of the body parts just mentioned. This might seem weird or disturbing at first, but get past the funkiness and truly think about what life would be like. Would you have to live at the hospital all the time? Would someone else have to take care of you? Could you get around at all? Would you even be alive?

body be good

As you do not know the path of the wind, or how the body is formed in a mother's womb, so you cannot understand the work of God, the Maker of all things.
Ecclesiastes 11:5

Have you ever thought about God's thought process when He was dreaming up bodies? In my imagination, I see God scratching His scruffy chin (He's been up for five days straight!) and humming the African-American slave spiritual "Dem Bones" to Himself:

> The Lord He thought He'd make a man.
> Dem bones gonna rise again!
> So He made Adam cordin' to a plan.
> Dem bones gonna rise again![1]

Then I picture Him busting out in a loud, Mary J. Blige-ish version of "Dry Bones," another slave spiritual, while all the angels back Him up with choreography and harmonies:

> Your toe bone connected to your foot bone.
> Your foot bone connected to your ankle bone.
> Your ankle bone connected to your leg bone.
> Your leg bone connected to your thigh bone.
> Your thigh bone connected to your hip bone.
> Your hip bone connected to your back bone.
> Your back bone connected to your shoulder bone.
> Your shoulder bone connected to your neck bone.
> Your neck bone connected to your head bone.
> Now hear the word of the Lord.[2]

That may not be how you imagine it. (Don't worry; I'm not *too* hurt.) But isn't it strange to think about the intricate design and engineering of your body? Take your nervous system, for example—your body's information gatherer, storage system and control center extraordinaire. Thousands and thousands of tiny nerves in every part of your body gather information about your surroundings, send that information through a network of neurons in your spine (kind of like a bunch of friends instant messaging each other) to your brain. Your brain then analyzes that information, decides the appropriate action to take and sends that message back through the neurons to your nerves and muscles, which respond immediately (such as pulling your hand away from a snapping dog). And it all happens in half a second or less.[3] Whether or not you imagine that God sang a Mary J. Blige version of "Dry Bones" as He knitted together the first human bodies, you have to give Him credit for being a creative genius. Half a second or less is *fast*.

God *had* to come up with a brilliant design for the human body, because His plan in creation all along was for people to be bearers of His image—and that's no easy task! We needed a body that could keep up with God's dreams for us, and that's exactly what we got.

put it in perspective

Do not be wise in your own eyes; fear the Lord and shun evil. This
will bring health to your body and nourishment to your bones.
Proverbs 3:7-8

Before we get too deep into talking about self-respect and loving your body, let's take a moment to consider how truly awesome it is to have a body—*any* body—at all. This crazy collection of skin, bones, muscles, blood and guts gives us the opportunity to be in God's world and to appreciate it with our minds and hearts. Think about some of the things you love in this beautiful world of ours, and then think about how you experience them through your five senses. Make a list. I've put down one of mine to get you started.

Sunshine. I love the way it feels on my skin!

You couldn't love any of these things if you didn't have a body to experience them. Even if you are disabled in a way that limits one of your senses—being deaf, for example—you are still able to enjoy God's creation because of your other senses. What a gift! Take a minute to write a prayer of thanksgiving for the intricate, amazing body that God has given you.

You'd think that the gift and blessing of a body would be enough, but God never stops at "enough." God multiplies the blessing by allowing us to have "dominion" over our bodies, which means that we have the authority and the free will to treat our bodies in whatever way we choose (see Genesis 1:28). This can be a good thing or a bad thing. We can choose to care for and treat our bodies with respect, or we can choose to abuse and treat our bodies with contempt (that means hatred).

The choice is ours. Take some time to think about this choice, and then write about how you would like to use the authority and free will God has given you over your body.

the body as it was meant to be

Come, let us bow down in worship, let us kneel before the LORD our Maker.
Psalm 95:6

God gave us these specially designed bodies as tools to live out the creative image of God in us. Through our bodies, we can experience the beauty God has created around us and worship Him for it; we can also *join* in His creative work! Our bodies give us the chance to draw, write, dance, sing, talk with friends, bake a cake, build spaceships and do just about anything else we can dream up. If we didn't have these bodies, we'd be very little help in God's ongoing creation project.

Don't forget that God invites us to be creative with our bodies too. The human body is like an artist's canvas, and we can join with the master Artist in making them beautiful. We can make creative choices about fashion, style, makeup and hair that will reflect God's creative image shining in and through us. Think big! Your morning beauty routine is a chance to work with the greatest Painter in the universe to make beauty—it's not just an attempt to make straw into gold.

We can literally show the world around us that God's image is in us, bursting to get out. Think about this change in perspective and how it might look in the real world, and then write your thoughts in the journal space provided. Sit down with your mom or a "big sis" and ask for her thoughts on this topic. Share your thoughts with her, and see if you can challenge each other to think big about revealing God's image to the world!

Notes
1. Author unknown, "Dem Bones," ScoutSongs.com Virtual Songbook. http://www.scoutsongs.com/lyrics/dembones.html (accessed December 2, 2004).
2. Author unknown, "Dry Bones," Hope College: Reading the Old Testament. http://www.hope.edu/academic/religion/bandstra/RTOT/CH12/BONES.HTM (accessed December 2, 2004).
3. "The Brain and Nervous System," Yahoo Health. October 4, 2004. http://health.yahoo.com/news/44393 (accessed January 12, 2005).

eight: IMPERFECT

Man looks at the outward appearance, but the LORD looks at the heart.
1 Samuel 16:7

Look, you and I both know there's more to life than *Cosmo, Allure* and *InStyle*. We both know that we're supposed to care about our inner beauty more than our outer beauty, our smarts more than our looks and our spirits more than our tushies and ta-tas. (That's good-girl code for "buns of steel" and "breasts of spectacular proportion.") We both know that the most important things in life aren't things at all—God, family, friends—but, let's get real.

We love fashion and beauty mags, and we hate them—all at the same time. We read them with a mix of fascination and horror. *You can see right through that dress!* (Envy and disgust.) *Look how skinny she is!* (Shock and awe.) *There's no way those things are real!* (Repulsion and curiosity.)

Do you ever wonder why we bother? I mean, we already know that, in the scope of eternity, it doesn't really matter that Diesel jeans are way cuter than BCBG's—right? We already know that being 5'11" and weighing 98 pounds can't be healthy—right? We already know, deep down, that what counts in the long run is the loving heart, mind and character that grow inside us as we grow closer to God.

So why do we look forward to pouring over the latest issue of *Glamour*?

the truth good and bad

(We already talked about this, but like leftover pizza, it's worth revisiting.) Good truth: We love beauty. God created us this way—on purpose. Our love of beauty is a reflection of His amazing creative Spirit that He imprinted on each one of our spirits. On purpose. No accident. Period.

Don't miss this! We love beauty and making ourselves beautiful because God's creative image is imprinted on our souls. It's okay to enjoy the beauty that surrounds us—even if it's in *Vogue*.

The problem comes when our love of beauty bumps up against a lot of other people's love of beauty—then nobody knows whose version of "beautiful" is right. And the bad truth, my lovely friend, is that the advertisers almost always win.

You may not believe this, but skinny has not always been the epitome of perfection. Not so very long ago, women would do absolutely *anything* to get fat. I'm not kidding. Here is a quote that I find a bit disturbing (and kind of hilarious), and you might too.

In just 4 weeks, I gained 39 pounds, a new womanly figure, and much needed fleshliness.[1]

I just love that she sounds so pleased with herself! This beauty-loving woman was quoted in an *advertisement* for a product that claimed it could make her fatter. The maker of this product—Professor Williams—wanted to sell more of his fat-enhancing merchandise, so he had a beautiful woman (by the standards of the day) use it and then testify to the amazing weight gain she experienced. The professor sold a *lot* of his stuff. Women were crazy about being huge. My point here is that we may *think* that our ideals of "beautiful" are completely independent of anyone else's, but they're probably not. From a very early age, images of "The Perfect Woman" bombard us, and we subconsciously start to accept those images pretty quickly.

ideals of beauty

Use the space below to describe what you think the perfect woman would look like. Or, if you're feeling really creative (I hope you are, by now!), plow through your favorite magazines, cut out pictures of the perfect woman, grab a glue stick and make a collage here or on a piece of construction paper.

My friend Jessie asked some of her high school girlfriends to describe *their* ideas of the perfect woman. Here are some of their answers:

"Blonde . . . tanned skin and thin."

"Thin . . . nice eyelashes and smile."

"Around 5'10" and wears clothes size 8 . . . [with] naturally long eyelashes."[2]

Did you notice anything? Pretty similar ideals, huh? And how do these answers compare with the ideal you came up with on page 58?

Now, you can choose to believe that we share similar ideas about the perfect woman because there really is an objective, genuine, all-time standard of perfection (and we've all found it on the cover of *Seventeen*), or you can go back and read about Professor Williams and the 39-pounds-gained-in-four-weeks woman and change your answer on page 58. Go ahead. I'll wait.

All kidding aside, our individual ideals about beauty have been squeezed and squished and nipped and tucked until we've got no original ideas left. It's tragic. It's scary.

reexamining your beauty

I'm willing to bet a million dollars (that I don't have, but I'm really sure about this) that there is something you hate (or at least strongly dislike) about your appearance. Just to get things rolling, I'll tell you mine.

I have a big butt—not a J. Lo, perky-and-round-and-looks-good-when-you-dance booty, but a wide, flat, weird-shaped butt. This butt is attached to large thighs. They're not super flabby, but they are *big*, baby. Even when I am in good shape (not now), my thighs are big—or *sturdy*, as I like to say when I'm feeling good about myself.

Okay, I told you mine. Now you tell me yours.

When you and I compare the things we hate about our appearance with our ideas of the perfect woman, we'll *always* come up short. Even celebrities have something they hate about their appearance. And the lame thing is, we're so preoccupied comparing the thing we hate with the ideal that *we miss the beauty that is already there.*

I'm beginning to suspect there is beauty to be found way, *way* outside of the ideal. To prove it to myself, I've started doing what I like to call "double takes" when I want to see the beauty that the ideal tells me isn't there. Here's how it works.

I catch sight of my hindquarters in a mirror or other reflective surface, such as a store window at the mall or a passing car driven by a gorgeous guy. My first thought—or "take"—is, *Good gravy! My rear looks like two loaves of bread having a tea party under a picnic blanket!* After I've gotten my initial reaction out of the way, I make myself take a second look at the tea-partying loaves of bread, even if I feel this will be truly painful. I make myself do a second take. When I look again, I do two things.

1. I see that my backside is the same backside my mom has, and my grandmother has, and my great-grandmother had before she passed away. I remember that this backside did not keep my mom from marrying a handsome and loving man, and it did not keep her from becoming a highly respected college professor and church minister. I remember that this backside did not keep my grandmother from marrying a handsome and loving man, and it did not keep her from living a long life, full of good friends and adventures around the world. I remember that this backside did not keep my great-grandmother from marrying a handsome and loving man, and it did not keep her from driving her four young daughters to California in a beat-up pickup during the Great Depression, after her husband died. I see the backside I inherited from these amazing women in a whole new light. This butt is going places.

2. I call to mind awesome words of God that I have memorized for just such an emergency. If you have not tucked away some key verses that remind you of God's love, care and celebration of your beauty, *start now*! As I have said before, God wants to speak to you through the gift of Scripture, and when your beauty is not the most obvious thing in the room, there's no better guy to hear from than God! Here are a few of my favorites:

> Let the beloved of the LORD rest secure in him, for he shields him all day long, and the one the LORD loves rests between his shoulders (Deuteronomy 33:12).

> As a father has compassion on his children, so the LORD has compassion on those who fear him; for he knows how we are formed, he remembers that we are dust (Psalm 103:13-14).

> I praise you because I am fearfully and wonderfully made; your works are wonderful, I know that full well (Psalm 139:14).

Sometimes I have to remind myself that God doesn't think I'm stupid for feeling as if I don't measure up. He understands, better than anyone in the universe, that sometimes my humanity gets the better of me. He is full of compassion and love, even in my most ridiculous moments.

So that's my double-take method for seeing the beauty that the perfect woman refuses to admit is there. My rump comes from a long, long line of successful rumps, and God loves my rump exactly the way it is. *That's* beautiful.

take the DOUBLE-TAKE
challenge

Now it's your turn. Using a mirror or other reflective surface, take a good, long look at the thing you hate about your appearance. Go ahead and allow yourself your first reaction—such as, "My skin looks like it could solve the worldwide oil crisis" or "I've seen bigger boobs on peewee football players." Then do a double take. See in the future of your greasy skin that you will not have one wrinkle until you're 97, or remind yourself that small boobs defy gravity much longer than big ones. (If you don't believe me, ask your mother or an older friend who won't mind.) Then dust off the trusty Word of God that you have so wisely memorized, and bask in the adoration of your creator. He sees your beauty, even when you don't.

And if you're a singer (or even if you're not), here's a little song to sing as part of your double-take. It was written by a truly beautiful girl named Kendall Payne, and you can hear it on her album *Grown*.

I don't care what anybody thinks
I will stare when everybody blinks
I don't mind the difference that they see
'Cause He loves every little thing . . .
Every little thing about me.[3]

Take the double-take challenge for a week and write down what you discover in the journal space below. Allow yourself to see the beauty that you didn't even know was there!

Notes

1. Linda Rellergert, "Body Image Advertising," *Missouri Families*, April 5, 2004.
   http://missourifamilies.org/features/nutritionarticles/nut43.htm (accessed October 25, 2004).
2. Jessie Minassian, informal survey conducted with three teenagers, December 2004.
3. Kendall Payne, "Little Things," *Grown*. Copyright 2004. Used by permission.
   Visit Kendall Payne at www.kendallpayne.com.

nine: expressive

In your anger do not sin; when you are on your beds, search your hearts and be silent.
Psalm 4:4

Our bodies offer us unlimited possibilities to express God's image, but they also offer the same chance to express our not-so-great parts. We all know that none of us is perfect, and sometimes our better halves take the day off. Being a teenager sometimes feels as if we're simmering pots of barely contained emotions, and occasionally, the pot done boileth over.

Sometimes it stinks being young. Not so long ago I browsed through some of my old journals from when I was in junior high. Here's a snippet of something I wrote in eighth grade:

> I hate the way Mom treats me like I'm a child. And she's not the only one. Everybody at church treats me like I'm five years old. They have no idea who I am, the things I think about. I hate that they don't think I can make my own decisions. They expect me to be this prim and proper "young lady" who agrees to everything they think is best for me. But I think I know what's best for me, and they never give me a chance to prove it. It's my life, but everybody keeps trying to live it for me.

Pretty bitter, huh? I was angry a lot, mostly about being in the in-between time: not a kid anymore, and not a grown-up yet. I felt grown-up a long time before everyone else started treating me like it. I felt as if I had to fight for control, especially with my parents. I couldn't wear the clothes I wanted to wear, I couldn't go to bed when I wanted to, I couldn't do the things I wanted to do, and I couldn't go to the places I wanted to go. I felt as if I were living a double life, as if I was this secret agent who everyone saw as a little kid on the outside but who was really a smart, mature and powerful woman on the inside. I wished that everybody could see who I really was.

Sound familiar? Are there times in your life when you're sure every adult on the planet is a part of some kind of conspiracy to keep you a kid? Use the space provided to write down some of your frustrations; or make a list of some "adult" things you think you're ready for but that the adults in your life aren't so sure of.

You may not be the angry young woman that I was, but you may have other overwhelming emotions that are difficult to express. Do you feel guilty sometimes, or misunderstood or abandoned? Maybe you feel unloved. Give yourself some uninterrupted time (at least a half hour) to express these feelings in writing. You can use the space below, or write in your own journal.

Recognizing the many emotions you're feeling and finding ways to express them are incredibly important. Sometimes it's hard to find words to wrap around such huge issues, but learning to communicate what's going on inside is the only healthy way to deal. If we don't talk, these emotions will find their way out in a destructive way—such as eating disorders, cutting and other bodily abuses.

eat your heart out

I am in distress; my eyes grow weak with sorrow, my soul and my body with grief.
Psalm 31:9

Refrain from anger and turn from wrath; do not fret—it leads only to evil.
Psalm 37:8

My disgrace is before me all day long, and my face is covered with shame.
Psalm 44:15

It's important to understand that eating disorders are not about food. *They are about emotion.* Sometimes emotions, such as guilt, neglect or anger, can *feel* physical (like a knot in your stomach or a lump in your throat), and eating disorders attempt to cover up those emotional feelings with real, physical feelings. Sometimes dealing with something physical seems a lot easier than dealing with something emotional. When I was 13, I felt angry and out of control, and instead of talking about and dealing with those feelings, I tried to get revenge and gain control by going hungry.

This is the case for most anorexics (people who starve themselves on purpose). Anorexia is about feeling angry and out of control, and trying to regain control in one small area of life: eating (or *not* eating, actually).

Bulimia, on the other hand, is often about guilt. Bulimics—people who binge on food and then "purge" by taking laxatives or vomiting—feel shame about something emotional, so they physically mirror that shame by doing something "naughty" (overeating) and then flush the guilt away as quickly as possible.

Compulsive overeating usually reflects an unmet emotional need such as attention, respect or recognition, which overeaters try to fill with the comfort of food. Girls who overeat may also have an unconscious (that means they're not aware of it) desire to be fat. They may feel unloved, so they create a "reason" for being unlovable.

I probably don't have to tell you of the real, physical dangers that come along with an eating disorder, but I'll hit a few highlights anyway. The risks of anorexia are obvious: starving yourself will kill you. Our bodies run on food, and they will eventually not run at all if they are denied fuel. Starving is a slow, ugly death in which everything—hair, skin and internal organs, to name a few—breaks down at a snail's pace, literally *becoming* the food that your body isn't getting. It's not pretty, and it's definitely not healthy.

Bulimia kills in exactly the same way, but with the added bonuses of serious digestive problems (a result of taking laxatives) and/or mouth and throat infections (a result of excessive vomiting). The acid from emptying your stomach on a regular basis burns away the lining of the throat, mouth and teeth, until there's nothing left. Yummy!

The hazards of compulsive overeating are more long-term but no less dangerous. Being overweight (which is an obvious result of overeating) results in heart, liver and intestinal disorders, as well as an increased risk of diabetes—a disease that limits your body's ability to process sugar. That may not sound terribly menacing, but do a search for "diabetes" on the Internet, and you'll see how bad it really is.[1]

So to sum it up, eating disorders outwardly reflect how we feel on the inside when we are unwilling or unable to honestly communicate our negative feelings. Girls who struggle with an eating disorder translate their difficult-to-deal-with emotions into an outlet that *seems* more manageable. But clearly, anorexia, bulimia and compulsive overeating come with their own complications.

Do you ever starve yourself, purge or overeat in an effort to feel in control of your life or to mask emotional pain? If so, talk about what drives you to do it and how you feel afterward. If these aren't struggles for you, write a prayer to God, asking Him to empower you to help your friends who struggle with eating disorders.

If you are dealing with a disorder of this kind, please don't try to solve it on your own! Talk to someone—such as your mom or dad, a church youth leader or a school counselor—and let him or her walk with you through the difficult times ahead. Then get your hands on a few of the many resources out there for girls who are trying to restore their physical — and emotional — health and wellness.

CUT TO THE QUICK

I am set apart with the dead, like the slain who lie in the grave,
whom you remember no more, who are cut off from your care.
Psalm 88:5

Another destructive way negative emotions boil to the surface is through cutting, or self-mutilation. Cutting is another way girls try to translate emotional pain into a more "manageable" physical pain. When their painful emotions and crushed heart feel like too much, cutters will scratch, burn or slice their skin in order to replace that emotional hurt with real, physical pain.

Girls who cut can start with any of the same negative emotions as those girls with eating disorders, such as anger, guilt or unfulfilled needs; but usually a cutter also struggles with self-hatred. She turns all the destructive feelings inward, toward her own spirit, which she doesn't feel is worth loving. She believes somewhere in her mind or her heart that she deserves to be in pain. If this is you, I'm telling you right now that it's a lie. God Himself has thumb-printed His image on your beautiful spirit, and nothing you do can stop Him from loving and adoring you.

Though you may have different reasons for cutting yourself, at the very root you are running away from feelings that you need to deal with in a healthy way. You must learn how to face those feelings and deal with those situations that cause you pain. Know that you are loved by creator God and that you are a reflection of His image. Cutting is physically, emotionally and spiritually destructive, and I pray that you will talk to a trustworthy adult as soon as possible and begin to heal, so that you can start to truly live. You are not alone, and you are loved!

express**yourself**

The mouth of the righteous man utters wisdom, and his tongue speaks what is just.
Psalm 37:30

There are endless ways that negative emotions seep out if they don't get expressed, such as bullying others, dressing inappropriately to get attention, rebelling against parents, compromising sexually, underachieving at school, having anxiety attacks or panic attacks, and the list goes on and on and on and *on*. The hard truth is that whatever is inside us will make its way out one way or another, and if we don't let it out in a healthy and mature way, it will break out in a damaging and harmful way.

💬 **How do you usually deal with the negative emotions you feel? For example, if your best friend said some really hurtful things about you that really made you mad, how would you deal?**

Feeling angry or sad or frustrated is not the problem. These emotions are valid, important and totally okay. They tell you when something isn't right. The problem arises when we don't recognize those feelings and/or don't express them in a healthy way. It's a two-step process: (1) recognition and (2) expression.

RECOGNITION

First you have to figure out what you're feeling. Writing in a journal about situations and your emotional reactions to them is a very smart way to work out your feelings. Writing in a journal will also give you time to cool down if you're raging or sobbing uncontrollably. (Maybe that's just me.) You can also draw how you're feeling; then try to describe what you see in words. Getting to a place where you can describe how you feel in words is very important, because words are the primary way that we communicate with others, which we'll discuss in step 2.

You may have noticed that all the Scripture verses in this chapter are from the book of Psalms. Psalms is an amazing example of people writing about their feelings—good, bad and just plain ugly! The writers of Psalms don't turn away from hard-to-deal-with emotions; they step right up and write a song about it. When you can't seem to put your finger on how you really feel, Psalms is a great read to get the juices flowing. You may be surprised at how honest these songs are! You may also want to write your own psalms—that's one of my favorite ways to let off steam and break down emotional chaos into understandable bits. Use the space below to write your own personal psalm, either now or the next time you need to sort through your feelings.

EXPRESSION

Now that you can kind of put your finger on how you're feeling, it's time to talk about it. If you have a conflict with your parents or a friend, sit down with them and express what you've discovered. Try to make statements about how *you're* feeling, instead of making accusations about their character or intentions. For example, "I feel angry about the fact that you won't let me go to see *Night of the Living Dead Part 15*. I think I'm old enough and mature enough," instead of, "You never let me do anything I want to do! You're the worst mother to ever walk the face of the earth!" I think you can see the difference.

After you've expressed your side of things, listen closely to how the other person responds, and make an effort to see the situation from his or her perspective. Exchange ideas and try to reach a compromise, and if the air starts to get heated, don't be afraid to take a break. Want to hear one of the wisest things someone has ever said to me? "In a week, you won't remember what the argument was about, but you will remember *how* you argued." If you can remember that, you'll be in good shape.

If your negative emotions arise from how you're feeling about *you*—rather than from a conflict with another person—it's still *mucho importante* (that's Spanish for "really blazing important") to talk it through with someone you trust, preferably someone older such as a parent, pastor or counselor. Express yourself! You are not alone, and there are people who love you who can help you face whatever is inside. Begin to let those things out, before they force their way out!

🗨 **The next time you're faced with fiery or painful emotions, what do you plan to do to recognize and express those feelings?**

Note
1. Mary Pipher, *Reviving Ophelia: Saving the Selves of Adolescent Girls* (New York; Ballantine Books, 1995), pp. 166-185.

ten: stylish

I love to shop. Show me three hours at the local outlet mall, and I will show you a very happy girl. I love the quest, the challenge of making my way through endless racks of rubbish to find that one perfect thing, that thing I have waited my entire life to find, that thing that will make my previously unremarkable existence magically transform into bliss. Or that's what it feels like anyway, when I finally stumble onto something I can actually afford and that does not make me look like a blimp or a Britney Spears wannabe.

My passion for shopping puts me in good company. Most of my girlfriends love to shop. In fact, I can count on one hand the number of women I have met in my lifetime who don't find "shopping therapy" an intensely uplifting experience. There are very few bad days that can't be saved by a trip to Target.

What's your favorite place to shop? What do you like about it? Do you like to go shopping with friends, family or by yourself? Use the space below to describe your idea of the perfect shopping trip.

Shopping inspires my imagination. When something cute catches my eye, I immediately start rummaging my closet in my head for anything that will match, assembling outfits out of thin air and trying them on in the privacy of my brain's fitting room. *Maybe this lime green camouflage sweater will go with those lavender jeans I bought at that garage sale last summer. No, I'd look like the Easter Bunny at war. Well, maybe with the red suede skirt from the Salvation Army thrift shop. No, too Christmassy. I know! It'll be perfect with Bryan's tweed suit, and he probably won't mind if I borrow it again. That's it! And for $11.99, it's a steal!*

STYLEFILE

Consequently, you are no longer foreigners and aliens, but fellow citizens with God's people and members of God's household, built on the foundation of the apostles and prophets, with Christ Jesus himself as the chief cornerstone (Ephesians 2:19-20).

You can probably tell from the fact that I would seriously consider wearing lavender jeans and lime-green camouflage at the same time that I have a strange sense of style. Now that I'm an adult, nobody seems to mind; but when I was growing up, no one knew what to think of me. I didn't seem to fit with the preppy kids, or the punks or the ghetto *fabulosos*. I liked bits and pieces from all of those fashions, but I put them together in ways that didn't make sense to anybody else. My wacky style made me hard to *stereotype*, which (in simple terms) is when we look at the outside of someone and make judgments about what's inside.

Have you ever thought about how much a person's clothes influence what we assume about them? No? Well, then, it's game time! It's time to play Let's Make a Stereotype! I will describe someone's clothes, and you tell me the "type" of person she is. Go with your first reaction, and write down the word you and your friends would use to describe these girls (such as "rock chick," "techi-geek," etc.), along with a few details like what music they're into or what they might do on a Friday night for fun. Okay, let's get started.

> • Contestant Number One is wearing holey, black-and-white-striped tights and combat boots with big buckles. Her black-lace miniskirt is frayed on the bottom; she has on several studded black-leather belts; and her torn, oversized T-shirt reads, "All Pop Stars Must Die." How would you stereotype Contestant Number One?

> • Contestant Number Two is wearing skin-tight lowrider jeans and her G-string underwear is peeking out from the top. Her belly-baring shirt is a size or three too small, and the four-inch stiletto heels she's teetering around on could be used as ninja weapons. How would you stereotype Contestant Number Two?

> • Contestant Number Three is wearing a long, flowing floral skirt and sandals, and she has several toe rings. She has a flower in her hair, and her natural-fiber denim jacket is embroidered with the command "Honor the Goddess Within." How would you stereotype Contestant Number Three?

Think for a few minutes about what you *think* you know about these three girls. Are you pretty sure you know why each girl chooses to dress the way she does? Do you think you know what is most important in each girl's life? How do you know, *really?* The truth is, how people choose to look on the outside can give us a lot of valuable information about them, but it never tells the whole story.

hearing the story

And why do you worry about clothes? See how the lilies of the field grow. They do not labor or spin. Yet I tell you that not even Solomon in all his splendor was dressed like one of these. If that is how God clothes the grass of the field, which is here today and tomorrow is thrown into the fire, will he not much more clothe you, O you of little faith?
Matthew 6:28-30

We can catch little glimpses of a person's story by observing the art of his or her personal style. But the minute we think we've got people figured out because of their cowboy hat or biker jacket, we forget the most important part of their story: the story of God's image in them.

The next time you find yourself stereotyping someone based on his or her style, take 30 seconds to look past the obvious and see if you can hear what they are trying to say *through* their style. Are they saying that they feel ignored and need attention? Are they saying that they feel scared and want to protect themselves? Are they saying that they feel unwanted yet want so bad to be desirable? Or they may be saying something positive, such as they feel confident, happy or free-spirited. How would people with these feelings dress? Can different styles say the same thing? What do you think?

Okay, time for some homework. Don't worry, it won't be *too* painful. Look at the people around you for two or three days, listening for what they might be saying through their style. Write or draw what you hear in the space provided; then find some time to talk about your observations with your mom or a "big sis."

telling the story

From Zion, perfect in beauty, God shines forth.
Psalm 50:2

Other people tell stories with their style, and guess what—you do, too! So what story do you want to tell? After you've spent some time observing what others are saying through their sense of style, start to think about what you would like to say.

> **Which of your characteristics, beliefs, talents, likes and dislikes would you like to express through what you wear? Do you want to tell the same story every day or change the story to fit your mood?**

I'm definitely a mood dresser. When I'm feeling playful, I choose bright colors and crazy prints. When I'm feeling down, I like to be cozy, so I wear my favorite hooded fleece sweatshirt. I also have a deep affection for the odd, so I sometimes wear one item that doesn't go with anything else I have on. That one little item, such as yellow socks or hot pink earrings, represents how I feel about my place in the world: I may not match, but at least I bring a little color!

● **How do you feel about your place in the world and what you have to offer as a bearer of God's creative image? How could you represent that in your style?**

Developing your own personal style can be intimidating at first, because all of us want to "fit in." But if you go back and read Ephesians 2:19-20 (it's on page 72, under "Style File"), you'll see that *all of us* "fit in!" When I was in school and people couldn't figure me out, it was scary at first. I was tempted to dress like everybody else just to make it easy on people who wanted to stereotype me. The longer I held out, though, the easier it got—and I actually had tons more friends because I refused to "fit in" with just one group. It was awesome!

As you gain confidence in letting the image of creator God shine through you, challenge yourself and your friends to be true to that image, instead of compromising your creativity to fit into a stereotype. Make a list of ways you will encourage others to express their personal style, instead of pressuring them to "fit in." How will you begin to celebrate your individuality and the uniqueness of others?

eleven: friendly

Amber Valletta, the world-famous supermodel, went to school at Booker T. Washington High School in Tulsa, Oklahoma. During her junior year, she was the cover model for *Seventeen*. Since then, she has appeared on countless magazine covers, starred in big-budget Hollywood movies, hosted MTV's *House of Style*, was Versace's model of the year and is now the face of Elizabeth Arden cosmetics.

Amber was a junior and on the cover of *Seventeen* the same year I was a freshman—at Booker T. Washington High School in Tulsa, Oklahoma. It was a rough year.

Ironically, it was the same year I discovered that green (with envy) is definitely not my best color.

Starting high school is hard enough without having one of the world's most beautiful women breezing by you in the hallway in her Guess? jeans, toting her books in a Prada bag, with a posse of hot guys trailing behind, sniffing her Calvin Klein perfume like a pack of rabid wolves. If I was lucky, I'd see her on a day when my one pair of thirdhand Guess? were clean, and I'd be walking with my one friend (which I prayed would make me appear cool and popular.) That night, I'd lock myself in the bathroom and spend three and a half hours trying to make my thick, wavy, mouse-brown hair look exactly like Amber's straight, perfectly highlighted honey-brown locks, using gel, mousse, spit, an ancient blow dryer and the sheer force of my will. It never worked.

You may not go to school with a future supermodel, but I'm confident that there's one girl in your school that you're envious of. Whether you go to a school with 50 students or 5,000, there is always one girl that every other girl wishes she would see looking back at her from the bathroom mirror. Use the space below to write about the girl you envy and—just for fun—be sure to describe all the things you resent about her. (Feel free to change her name, if you're paranoid someone might accidentally read this and pass it on to her.)

dealing with it

A heart at peace gives life to the body, but envy rots the bones.
Proverbs 14:30

And I saw that all labor and all achievement spring from man's envy of his neighbor.
This too is meaningless, a chasing after the wind.
Ecclesiastes 4:4

These verses are pretty straight up about God's attitude about envy. He's not a fan. Envy does two things that would make God cranky, if He were the type to get cranky (which He totally isn't).

Number one, envy blinds you to the beauty God has handpicked for you to possess. Each one of us bears a fingerprint of His glory, a slice of His creative image, which no one else has ever had in all of history, and no one else will ever have again. If we're busy longing for someone else's slice, we won't make much of our own.

Number two, envy keeps you from seeing the person you envy as a fellow image bearer. God imprinted His image on Amber Valletta, and instead of looking for that image, I was looking for a hairbrush. I never bothered to find out that Amber wanted to be a social worker when she grew up, or that she had a passion for homeless people. (Amber has since gone on to organize an annual fashion event that benefits the Tulsa Community Food Bank.) I was so busy wishing I had Amber's hair, jeans, bag and boys that I couldn't see her best accessory: the image of God—just like me.

Think back to the person you described in the previous section, the person who has it all. Now describe her in terms of God's image imprinted in her. In other words, describe her as God would describe her to someone who has never met or seen her.

jealousy
the nastier side of envy

Sometimes people mistakenly use the words "jealousy" and "envy" interchangeably, but they are almost opposites. "Envy" is the feeling you get when someone else has something you want. One usage of the word "jealousy" is a reference to the feeling you get when you've got something someone else wants and you don't want to share.

Amber Valletta wasn't the only extraordinary person I went to school with at Booker T. There was also Debbie. Debbie was . . . ugly. I'd like to use some other, nicer word, but "ugly" is the most accurate description, so I'll use it here (even though I feel really guilty.)

Debbie was probably about 6'2", but she had a hunched back, so hunched that her head did not get anywhere near the doorframe when she limped into the room. She had thick, Coke-bottle eyeglasses, her eyes were a bit out of kilter; and I'm not sure even braces could have done much for her teeth. She also had a speech impairment that wasn't exactly a lisp; it sounded more like she had cotton balls tucked in her cheeks. And if that wasn't enough, Debbie stuttered.

On one hand, I felt really bad for Debbie. She didn't have any friends, and if I happened to accidentally look her in the eye, she stared back at me with such heartbreaking hope that I might be her first one that I couldn't look away fast enough.

On the other hand, I was way too cool for Debbie. (Or so I thought, anyway.) I mean, I had my one friend; and although I often wished that I had a whole army of friends to equip myself for the battle of high school, when I looked at Debbie, my one friend seemed like more than enough. My social schedule's packed, sweetie. Sorry.

I guarded my (imaginary) reputation *jealously* from Debbie.

You may not go to school with someone like Debbie, but I'm confident there's one girl that you are so glad you're *not*. Whether you go to a school with 50 students or 5,000, there is one girl that every other girl has nightmares about seeing in a bathroom mirror. Use the space below to write about the girl you are too cool for, from whom you jealously guard your reputation like it's a bank vault. (Please, *please* change her name, because I am paranoid someone will accidentally read this and pass it on to her.)

dealing with it

Anger is cruel and fury overwhelming, but who can stand before jealousy?
Proverbs 27:4

Do nothing out of selfish ambition or vain conceit, but in humility consider others better than yourselves. Each of you should look not only to your own interests, but also to the interests of others. Your attitude should be the same as that of Christ Jesus.
Philippians 2:3-5

God feels much the same about jealousy as He does about envy—He's not a fan. Jealousy does two things that would make God cranky, if He were the type to get cranky (which, as I said before, He totally isn't).

Number one, jealousy disfigures the beauty God has handpicked for you. Nobody looks their best when they're ticked off, but Proverbs 27:4 says that jealousy is even uglier. You can't reflect God's glory when you refuse to share His glory. Your slice of God's image will always shine brightest when it's shared!

Number two, jealousy keeps you from seeing the people who aren't cool as fellow image bearers. God imprinted His image on Debbie, and instead of looking for that image, I was looking after my nonexistent reputation. I never bothered to find out *anything* about Debbie's interests, such as what she wanted to do when she grew up. And since she didn't become famous, I have no idea if her dreams came true. I was so busy avoiding any contact with Debbie that I never got close enough to see her best feature: the image of God—just like me.

> **Think back to the person you described in the previous section who doesn't seem to have much at all. Now describe her in terms of God's image imprinted in her. In other words, describe her as God would describe her to someone who has never met or seen her.**

acknowledging
God's "Other" Image

Now that we can admit that we all bear the fingerprint of God's creative image, we have to start thinking and acting like it—which is a lot easier than it sounds, especially when confronted with a supermodel or a misshapen giant standing by your locker.

Remember the Double-Take Challenge? Well, there's a part 2. In part 2, instead of taking a second look at yourself, start doing a double take when you look at others. Allow yourself your first reaction (such as "I wish I had Amber's life," or "I wish Debbie would get a life.") Then do a double take. Look past your feelings of envy or jealousy, and see the Ambers and the Debbies in your life as bearers of the very image of God, chosen by Him to carry a reflection of His glory. As you begin to see it, try to find ways to embrace and encourage those girls—and others around you—to let that image shine. The funny thing is, as you begin to see people this way, *your* beauty shines through!

Take part 2 of The Double-Take Challenge for a week, and write down what you discover in the journal space below. Begin to see and acknowledge the true beauty in others that you didn't even know was there!

twelve: glowing

I have a confession to make.

I'm not an expert in anything having to do with beauty. I spend about 10 minutes a day (combined) on my hair and makeup, and I would wear torn jeans and my fleece sweatshirt every day, if I thought I could get away with it. I shave my legs about once a week (that's being optimistic), exercise too rarely and have a passion for cheeseburgers that frightens me.

Now that you know the truth about me, you should also know that I love feeling beautiful—I just don't have a lot of time or patience to invest in the process. Through years of experimentation, I have figured out a few beauty shortcuts that at least make me look like I made an effort. In fact, I'm fairly sure that if you asked the people at my work or church whether they think I am beautiful, most would say yes. The only reason I feel qualified to talk about caring for and making the most of your beauty is that I have successfully been fooling people for years. I have discovered a few nonnegotiable beauty tips, and I am happy to share them with you.

Along with the beauty tips, I have included some verses from the Bible that will make your morning when you see them around your mirror as you're getting ready for the day. Grab some colored paper and glitter pens and adorn your bathroom or bedroom with these love notes to you from God. Sometimes we all need a little reminder about the beauty inside that wants to bust out!

hygiene queen

Who may ascend the hill of the LORD? Who may stand in his holy place?
He who has clean hands and a pure heart.
Psalm 24:3-4

My grandmother used to say, "Cleanliness is next to godliness." I have no idea whether this is true, but I do know that it is hard to see beauty through dirt and funk. The number one beauty nonnegotiable is, If it's attached to you, clean it. Brush and floss those pearly whites, scrape the goo from under your nails, put some Q-Tips to good use in your ears, and by all means, use deodorant! Everybody knows who the smelly kid is at school. Don't be the smelly kid!

This may seem obvious, but I can't tell you how many girls I've met who spend an hour on their makeup every day yet have nasty, yellow wax oozing out of their ears. Being clean and nice-smelling is the starting point for all the other beauty maximizing you might do. Like I said, if it's attached to you, clean it. Make a list below of some things you will do in the next week to be a cleaner you.

FACE IT

Those who look to him are radiant; their faces are never covered with shame.
Psalm 34:5

Wisdom brightens a man's face and changes its hard appearance.
Ecclesiastes 8:1

In Scripture, a person's face is an indicator of what's going on inside. When it's something good, you will read about faces being "radiant" or "bright." When it's something not so good, you'll read about faces being "downcast." Since your face is one of the ways other people see inside you, taking good care of it will let your beauty shine through.

The number two nonnegotiable is *not* makeup; it's skin care. If you spend tons of money and time covering up everything that's wrong with your skin, I promise your skin will only get worse. Your face will be with you for the rest of your life, so it's best to start treating it nicely while you can still make friends with it.

You probably know the basics of skin care, having learned them from all the magazines we love so much, but I'll share my method anyway: Wash gently twice a day; follow with a gentle toner; then moisturize, moisturize, moisturize. Preferably, use a moisturizer with sunscreen—*especially* if you have fair skin. Even if you have super oily skin, moisturize! If you leave your skin dry and stiff, it will produce even *more* oil, and soon you will be engaged in a (losing) battle with your confused and abused face.

When it comes to zits and blackheads, again, be gentle! The last thing you want is to trade in your temporary blemish for a permanent scar, so avoid picking and squeezing as much as possible. Try using a mild, exfoliating scrub once or twice a week, followed by a pore-shrinking masque. Zits form when dirt and crud get in your pores, so the trick is to keep them squeaky clean and sealed up tight (moisturizer again!)

💬 **How do you currently care for your face and the skin that covers it? What do you think you should start doing differently?**

As far as makeup is concerned, keep it simple. The whole point is to let your beauty shine through, and it's pretty hard for anything to peek through a layer of cement! Make sure your powder or foundation is a good match for your skin tone; then have fun experimenting with different eye shadows and lip colors. Be creative! You are imprinted with God's creative spirit. (But also get a second opinion from your mom or a "big sis" before you step out of the house.) Use the space below to list some of your favorite makeup dos and don'ts, and in the next week or so, take a survey of your friends' favorites. Sharing your ideas will make all of you more beautiful!

Stop-and-Stare Hair

How beautiful you are, my darling! Oh, how beautiful! Your eyes behind your veil are doves. Your hair is like a flock of goats descending from Mount Gilead.
Song of Songs 4:1

Hair is one of the ways I trick people into thinking I invest a lot of time and energy in my appearance. Here's the secret: Have your hair cut in a style that fits with the amount of time you're going to spend on it. Some styles demand more attention than others, so talk to your stylist about how much time you want to invest every morning.

Personally, I have short hair that looks messed up on purpose. It takes me all of 30 seconds to style in the morning, and I can't really have a bad hair day, since it always looks a tad on the wild side. It changes color a lot, mainly because I get bored easily and short-haired people are somewhat limited when we want to change it up a bit. Your parents may or may not be cool with your dying your hair every color of the rainbow. If they're not, respect their wishes—don't fight about it, and don't freak. You will have plenty of years after you're out of the house to get crazy with your locks. (Trust me—the first time I dyed my hair I was 19, seven years after I asked the first time. It was worth the wait.) If your parents are okay with your changing colors, be smart. Don't use Kool-Aid, peroxide or something weird. Remember that you have to live with the results, or pay to get any mistakes fixed. It's better to save up your allowance or get an extra babysitting job and do it right the first time.

As with our skin, "clean" and "moisturized" should describe our hair. Find a shampoo that will get out whatever styling gunk you put in but that does not strip your hair. You may have to try several to get the right balance. Samples at the drugstore are a good way to go. Follow up with a conditioner that will put good stuff in (vitamins, etc.) but won't build up. Again, get your hands on some samples.

Long hair beauty tip: Don't brush your hair when it's wet. Instead use a comb or pick. Start at the tips, working your way back to your scalp. This will help prevent breakage and split ends.

Short hair beauty tip: Get a cut every four or five weeks. Short hair loses its style and shape much faster than long hair, and you don't want to look like a shaggy beast.

DIET, SCHMIET!

These all look to you to give them their food at the proper time. When you give it to them, they gather it up; when you open your hand, they are satisfied with good things.
Psalm 104:27-28

Life is more than food . . . Who of you by worrying can add a single hour to [her] life?
Luke 12:23,25

Dieting is dangerous. Thirty percent of teenage girls who diet spend their adult life battling obesity. (Obesity is when you are 50 or more pounds over a healthy weight for your age and body type.) When you are a teenager, your body is changing a lot. (You may have noticed!) It's not only pouring hormones into your bloodstream to make you into a woman, but it's also trying to find the perfect balance between your height and weight. If you start trying to manipulate this process while your body is changing so rapidly—by going on the Zone or the South

Beach Diet, for instance—your metabolism (how your body burns and uses food) can be damaged and may not bounce back. Your body is designed to find its own balance—really! This may take a few years, and waiting for all the curves to get in the right place can be murder, but all your body needs from you during this process—and the rest of your life—is a little TLC (i.e., tender loving care).

TLC does *not* mean taking diet pills, "health" supplements or laxatives, and it does *not* mean trying one fad diet after another. TLC *does* means feeding your body good food that fuels its engines and helps it run efficiently. Obviously, fast food and junk food are not the way to get it done. Your body was ingeniously designed by God to run best on foods that He has created. Fresh is best! Fruits and vegetables and whole grains (such as wheat bread, oat bran and brown rice) are like high-performance gas to your body's engine, and two or three servings of protein (such as chicken, fish, beef and eggs) a day will help you build strong muscles and iron-rich blood.

Now, a slice of pizza or a bowl of Ben & Jerry's once in a while will not kill you, and as long as healthy foods are your normal fare, you shouldn't feel guilty for the occasional indulgence. As long as you practice moderation and self-discipline, enjoying high-fat, high-sugar treats is part of the joy of having taste buds (which God gave us). Just don't let those treats become a significant part of your regular food intake.

What do you think? On a scale of 1 to 10, how healthy are the foods you choose to eat on a normal day?

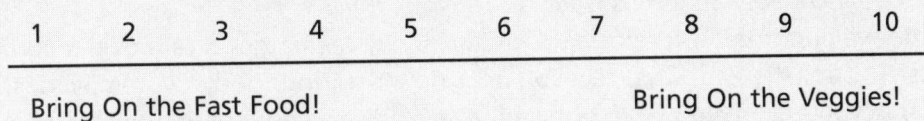

1	2	3	4	5	6	7	8	9	10

Bring On the Fast Food!   Bring On the Veggies!

If you feel that you have a weight problem, I recommend that you talk to your doctor. He or she will be honest with you about your health and can advise you how to *healthfully* manage your weight, without screwing up your metabolism beyond repair. Looking healthy is great, but *feeling* healthy and *being* healthy are far more important.

What are some ways you can eat more healthfully? Are you constantly worried about counting calories and losing weight? In the space below, write down your thoughts about your body size and shape, and then brainstorm with your mom, a "big sis" or a friend about how you can encourage each other to be healthy *and* love your beautiful bodies, whatever size they are!

run for the prize

Do you not know that in a race all the runners run, but only one gets the prize? Run in such a way as to get the prize. Everyone who competes in the games goes into strict training. They do it to get a crown that will not last; but we do it to get a crown that will last forever.
1 Corinthians 9:24-25

Forgetting what is behind and straining toward what is ahead, I press on toward the goal to win the prize for which God has called me heavenward in Christ Jesus.
Philippians 3:13-14

For many of us, the "prize" has always been a tight, toned body that will have cute boys falling in the street and other chicks wanting to strangle us. But if we are going to start living up to the image of God imprinted on our hearts, we need to rethink the ultimate prize. We are told in Proverbs, "Beauty is fleeting; but a woman who fears the Lord is to be praised" (Proverbs 31:30). Clearly, God has a higher agenda than buns of steel.

Our bodies are a gift from our creative God. They allow us to touch, see, hear, smell and taste the beauty He has created for our pleasure and to interact with others who are imprinted with His image. Our bodies also give us the opportunity to outwardly display the image of God in us—creativity— through hairstyles, makeup and fashion. Our bodies are an incredibly generous gift from an incredibly generous God.

So how do we honor the gift and thank the giver? By taking good care of the bodies He has given us! The apostle Paul says, "Do you not know that your body is a temple of the Holy Spirit, who is in you, whom you have received from God? You are not your own; you were bought at a price. Therefore honor God with your body" (1 Corinthians 6:19-20). The prize we should be seeking is *bringing honor to God*.

> **Just so we're clear, write down several things that you could do with your body that *wouldn't* honor God. Take a minute to think about it before you start writing.**

Regular exercise is an important part of honoring God with your body; it's a way to show Him how grateful you are for such an amazing gift. If your mom or dad gave you a brand-new Porsche for your birthday, I'm hoping you wouldn't slash the tires, key the paint and bash in the taillights with a sledgehammer. (If you *would* treat your $80,000 car like this, please e-mail me—I'd be happy to take that Porsche off your hands.) No, you'd baby that thing like it was your firstborn child, and you'd let your parents know a thousand times a day how thankful you were for such an awesome gift.

Well, I think you see my point. Exercise strengthens, energizes and keeps your body functioning at its peak, allowing you to do all the things God created for you to do. A good workout should include cardiovascular exercise (anything that gets your heart and blood pumping faster than normal) and strength training (like weight lifting or intensive stretching) to build your muscles. Ideally, you should work out three to four times a week.

Now just because you hear the term "work out," don't think you have to turn into a gym buff. There are a ton of ways to get good, regular exercise. Going to the gym is obvious, but it can be expensive. And if you don't drive yet, you'll always have to bug somebody to taxi you over there. Be creative! Go for a bike ride, take a hike, or invest in a dance class or some good workout DVDs. Grab a friend and brainstorm how you can exercise together. How will the two of you begin to run for the prize this week? Make a list of a few things that you can do to honor God with your amazing body. That way you'll have a bunch of ideas to pick from when you're ready to get out and use that amazing body God has given you.

My Exercise Ideas:

CARE COVENANT

You open your hand and satisfy the desires of every living thing.
The LORD is righteous in all his ways and loving toward all he has made.
The LORD is near to all who call on him, to all who call on him in truth.
Psalm 145:16-18

Time for another confession: After reading over this chapter, I'm feeling pretty funky about not caring very well for the body God's given me. I seem to forget too easily how cool it is that God has shaped me in His image! If you're like me, and want to make a commitment to honor God with your body, you can copy the covenant (promise) below and post it in a place where you'll see it every day. Or write your own covenant, committing to our creative and loving God that you will treat your body like the incredible gift that it is, and let His image in you shine to everyone with eyes to see it.

> Thank You, Lord, for my body that allows me to touch, see, hear, smell and taste Your beautiful creation. It's a generous and overwhelming gift! I want to run for the prize of honoring You with this body, and I covenant with You to care for it, so that Your image in me will shine brightly to everyone around.

Signed _____ Date _____

Soul Sister Leader Tips

*"Their leader will be one of their own; their ruler will arise from among them.
I will bring him near and he will come close to me, for who is he who will
devote himself to be close to me?" declares the LORD.*
Jeremiah 30:21

Whether this is your first time leading a group or you're a seasoned veteran, we're glad you've decided to embrace the challenge. You may be a mom, mentor or even a young woman yourself, but if God has called you to invest time, energy and emotion into the lives of young women, He will make your sacrifice well worth it!

The Soul Sister series can be done alone, with a "big sis" (mentor), with your mom or with one or more friends. If you are leading a group through these workbooks, your primary roles will be to organize a meeting time and to facilitate how you spend that time. We've put together a few tips to assist you in the process.

Suggestions for Group Study:

1. Do your best to make the environment conducive to talking about the areas in the girls' lives that hinder them from growing spiritually and from finding their identity. Stress the importance of confidentiality—what is shared stays within the group.

2. Before each meeting, read through the session and mark questions and sections that you think particularly apply to your group. During the meeting, don't spend too much time on one section unless it is obvious that God is working in people's lives at a particular moment. We all lead very busy lives; respect group members by beginning and ending meetings on time.

3. Make time for fun! If you find your group gets antsy easily, utilize the bulk of the time on activities, creative exercises and fellowship. Remember that relationships will be the most important thing these girls will take away from your group time.

4. You can't stress enough the importance of writing in a journal! This simple exercise will help the girls process their thoughts, apply what they're learning and leave a record of how far they've come.

5. Always begin and end the meetings with prayer. If your group is small, have the whole group pray together. If it is larger than 10 members, form groups of 2 to 4 to share and pray for one another.

6. Be prepared. Pray for your preparation and for the girls in your group during the week.

7. Don't let one person dominate the discussion. Ask God to help you draw out the quiet ones without putting them on the spot.

8. Spend time each meeting worshiping God, either at the beginning or end of the meeting. Don't be nervous! If you feel uncomfortable leading the group with an instrument, utilize worship CDs or invite one or more girls to lead everyone in worship.

Suggestions for Mentoring Relationships

As stated earlier, this workbook lends itself for use in mentoring relationships. Women, in particular, are admonished in Scripture to train younger women (see Titus 2:3-5). Some of the following suggestions might help you consider starting a mentoring relationship:

- A mentoring relationship could be arranged through a system set up by a church or youth ministry.
- If you'd like to mentor a younger woman or be mentored by someone who exemplifies a Christlike lifestyle, don't be shy! Mentoring doesn't have to be a formal process. Take the initiative and ask if you can meet every so often to go through this workbook together. More often than not, the relationship you build will far outlast the pages contained in this book.
- Don't shy away from mentoring simply because your walk with the Lord is less than perfect. We're all in process! God has commanded us to disciple new and growing believers, and He doesn't stipulate how "mature" we must be to mentor another. Don't worry— Matthew 28:20 says that God promises to be with you through thick and thin.
- Once you agree to mentor a young woman, be prepared to learn as much or more than she does! You will both be blessed by the mentoring relationship built on the relationship you have together in the Lord.

More Breakthrough Books from Soul Sister and Soul Survivor

Connect
The Lowdown on Relationships and Friendships
Kendall Payne
ISBN 08307.37316

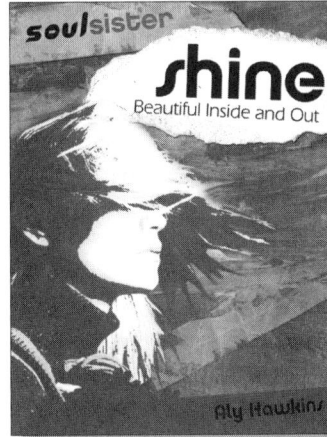

Shine
Beautiful Inside and Out
Aly Hawkins
ISBN 08307.37308

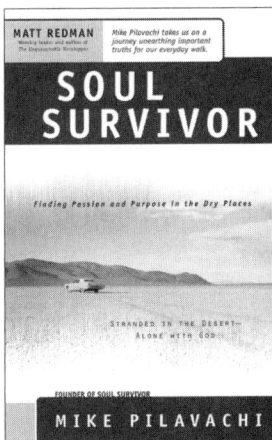

Soul Survivor
Finding Passion and Purpose in the Dry Places
Mike Pilavachi
ISBN 08307.33248

Soul Sister
The Truth About Being God's Girl
Beth Redman
ISBN 08307.32128